50 Best Steak Dishes for the House

By: Kelly Johnson

Table of Contents

- Classic Ribeye Steak
- Filet Mignon with Garlic Butter
- New York Strip Steak
- T-Bone Steak
- Porterhouse Steak
- Flank Steak with Chimichurri
- Skirt Steak Fajitas
- Grilled Hanger Steak
- Tomahawk Steak
- Denver Steak with Herb Sauce
- Cajun Blackened Steak
- Steak au Poivre
- Philly Cheesesteak
- Steak Diane
- Korean BBQ Beef Steak
- Carne Asada
- Peppercorn Crusted Steak

- Coffee-Rubbed Steak
- Chimichurri Flank Steak
- Garlic Butter Basted Steak
- Asian Marinated Steak
- Blue Cheese Crusted Steak
- Herb-Crusted Sirloin
- Stuffed Flank Steak
- Surf and Turf
- Balsamic Glazed Steak
- Grilled Ribeye with Rosemary
- Mushroom Sauce Steak
- Teriyaki Glazed Steak
- Steak Salad with Arugula
- Classic Steak Sandwich
- Jamaican Jerk Steak
- Red Wine Braised Steak
- Mediterranean Steak Skewers
- Wasabi Crusted Steak
- Steak with Béarnaise Sauce

- Pepper Steak Stir Fry
- Garlic and Thyme Steak
- Grilled Flat Iron Steak
- Steak Tacos
- Asian Beef Bulgogi Steak
- Montreal Smoked Steak
- Spicy Chipotle Steak
- Lemon Garlic Steak
- Herb Butter Sirloin
- Japanese Wagyu Steak
- Black Garlic Butter Steak
- Coffee and Chili Rubbed Steak
- Rosemary Garlic Ribeye
- Truffle Butter Steak

Classic Ribeye Steak

Ingredients:

- 1 ribeye steak (1–1.5 inches thick)
- Salt and freshly ground black pepper
- 2 tbsp olive oil
- 2 cloves garlic, smashed
- 2 sprigs fresh rosemary or thyme

Instructions:

1. Let steak come to room temperature. Season generously with salt and pepper.
2. Heat a cast iron skillet over high heat with olive oil until smoking.
3. Sear steak 4–5 minutes per side for medium-rare, adding garlic and herbs halfway through.
4. Rest 5 minutes before slicing and serving.

Filet Mignon with Garlic Butter

Ingredients:

- 2 filet mignon steaks
- Salt and pepper
- 2 tbsp olive oil
- 3 tbsp butter
- 3 garlic cloves, smashed
- Fresh thyme sprigs

Instructions:

1. Season steaks with salt and pepper. Heat oil in skillet over medium-high heat.
2. Cook steaks 3–4 minutes per side for medium-rare.
3. Add butter, garlic, and thyme to pan. Spoon melted butter over steaks for 1–2 minutes.
4. Rest and serve.

New York Strip Steak

Ingredients:

- 1 New York strip steak
- Salt and pepper
- 1 tbsp vegetable oil
- 1 tbsp butter

Instructions:

1. Season steak well with salt and pepper.
2. Heat oil in pan until shimmering. Sear steak 4 minutes per side for medium-rare.
3. Add butter at the end, baste steak for flavor. Rest before serving.

T-Bone Steak

Ingredients:

- 1 T-bone steak (1–1.5 inches thick)
- Salt, pepper, olive oil

Instructions:

1. Bring steak to room temp and season well.
2. Grill over high heat 4–5 minutes per side for medium-rare.
3. Let rest 5 minutes, slice and serve.

Porterhouse Steak

Ingredients:

- 1 Porterhouse steak
- Salt, pepper, olive oil

Instructions:

1. Season steak and bring to room temperature.
2. Grill or pan-sear on high heat 5–6 minutes per side for medium-rare.
3. Rest before slicing. Porterhouse has a larger tenderloin side than T-bone.

Flank Steak with Chimichurri

Ingredients:

- 1.5 lbs flank steak
- Salt and pepper

Chimichurri Sauce:

- 1 cup parsley
- 3 garlic cloves
- 2 tbsp red wine vinegar
- 1/2 cup olive oil
- 1 tsp oregano
- 1/2 tsp red pepper flakes
- Salt to taste

Instructions:

1. Grill steak 4–5 minutes per side. Rest and slice thinly against the grain.
2. Blend chimichurri ingredients and spoon over steak before serving.

Skirt Steak Fajitas

Ingredients:

- 1 lb skirt steak
- 1 onion, sliced
- 1 bell pepper, sliced
- 2 tbsp lime juice
- 1 tbsp olive oil
- 1 tsp chili powder, cumin, garlic powder
- Salt and pepper

Instructions:

1. Marinate steak with lime juice, oil, and spices 30 minutes.
2. Sear steak 3-4 minutes per side. Rest and slice thin.
3. Sauté onions and peppers. Serve with tortillas.

Grilled Hanger Steak

Ingredients:

- 1 lb hanger steak
- Salt, pepper, olive oil
- 2 cloves garlic, minced
- 1 tbsp fresh rosemary

Instructions:

1. Season steak with salt, pepper, garlic, and rosemary.
2. Grill over high heat 4 minutes per side for medium-rare.
3. Let rest and slice thinly.

Tomahawk Steak

Ingredients:

- 1 Tomahawk ribeye (2–3 lbs)
- Salt and pepper
- 2 tbsp olive oil
- 3 garlic cloves, smashed
- Fresh rosemary or thyme sprigs

Instructions:

1. Let steak come to room temp. Generously season with salt and pepper.
2. Preheat oven to 375°F (190°C).
3. Sear steak in a hot cast iron pan with olive oil, garlic, and herbs for 3–4 minutes each side.
4. Transfer pan to oven and roast 10–15 mins for medium-rare. Rest 10 mins before slicing.

Denver Steak with Herb Sauce

Ingredients:

- 1 Denver steak (about 1 inch thick)
- Salt and pepper
- 2 tbsp olive oil

Herb Sauce:

- 1/4 cup fresh parsley
- 2 tbsp chives
- 1 tbsp lemon juice
- 1/4 cup olive oil
- Salt and pepper

Instructions:

1. Season steak, heat oil in pan, and cook 4 minutes per side for medium-rare. Rest.
2. Blend herbs, lemon juice, olive oil, salt, and pepper until smooth.
3. Serve steak topped with herb sauce.

Cajun Blackened Steak

Ingredients:

- 2 ribeye or sirloin steaks
- 2 tbsp Cajun seasoning
- 1 tbsp butter
- Salt

Instructions:

1. Rub steaks with Cajun seasoning.
2. Heat cast iron pan until very hot, sear steaks 3–4 mins per side.
3. Add butter and baste before resting and serving.

Steak au Poivre

Ingredients:

- 2 filet mignon or strip steaks
- Salt and cracked black peppercorns
- 2 tbsp butter
- 1/4 cup brandy or cognac
- 1/2 cup heavy cream

Instructions:

1. Press peppercorns into steaks, season with salt. Sear in butter 4 mins per side. Remove steaks.
2. Deglaze pan with brandy (careful if flambéing).
3. Add cream, reduce until thickened.
4. Return steaks to pan briefly, then serve with sauce.

Philly Cheesesteak

Ingredients:

- 1 lb thinly sliced ribeye
- 1 onion, sliced
- 1 green bell pepper, sliced
- 4 hoagie rolls
- 8 slices provolone cheese
- Salt, pepper, oil

Instructions:

1. Sauté onion and pepper until soft.
2. Cook beef in batches, season. Combine with veggies.
3. Layer cheese to melt and stuff into rolls.

Steak Diane

Ingredients:

- 2 sirloin or filet steaks
- 2 tbsp butter
- 2 tbsp shallots, minced
- 1 clove garlic, minced
- 1/4 cup brandy
- 1/2 cup beef broth
- 1 tsp Dijon mustard
- 2 tbsp heavy cream
- Salt and pepper

Instructions:

1. Sear steaks 3–4 mins per side, set aside.
2. Sauté shallots and garlic in butter, deglaze with brandy.
3. Add broth, mustard, and cream; simmer until sauce thickens.
4. Return steaks to sauce, coat well, then serve.

Korean BBQ Beef Steak (Bulgogi Style)

Ingredients:

- 1 lb thinly sliced ribeye
- 1/4 cup soy sauce
- 2 tbsp sugar
- 2 tbsp sesame oil
- 4 garlic cloves, minced
- 1 tbsp grated ginger
- 2 green onions, sliced
- 1 tsp black pepper

Instructions:

1. Marinate beef in all ingredients for 30 mins.
2. Grill or pan-fry on high heat 2–3 mins per side. Serve with rice and kimchi.

Carne Asada

Ingredients:

- 1.5 lbs skirt or flank steak
- Juice of 2 limes
- 3 garlic cloves, minced
- 1/4 cup cilantro, chopped
- 1/4 cup olive oil
- 1 tsp cumin
- 1 tsp chili powder
- Salt and pepper

Instructions:

1. Marinate steak with all ingredients for at least 1 hour.
2. Grill on high heat 4–5 mins per side.
3. Let rest, slice thinly, serve with tortillas, salsa, and guacamole.

Peppercorn Crusted Steak

Ingredients:

- 2 steaks (ribeye or filet)
- 2 tbsp coarsely cracked black peppercorns
- Salt
- 2 tbsp olive oil
- 2 tbsp butter

Instructions:

1. Press cracked peppercorns firmly into both sides of steaks; season with salt.
2. Heat olive oil in a skillet over medium-high heat. Sear steaks 4 minutes per side for medium-rare.
3. Add butter, spoon melted butter over steaks for 1–2 minutes. Rest before serving.

Coffee-Rubbed Steak

Ingredients:

- 2 steaks (sirloin, ribeye)
- 1 tbsp finely ground coffee
- 1 tbsp brown sugar
- 1 tsp smoked paprika
- 1 tsp chili powder
- 1 tsp salt
- 1/2 tsp black pepper
- 2 tbsp olive oil

Instructions:

1. Mix coffee, sugar, paprika, chili powder, salt, and pepper. Rub onto steaks.
2. Heat oil in pan or grill, cook steaks 4–5 minutes per side for medium-rare. Rest before serving.

Chimichurri Flank Steak

Ingredients:

- 1.5 lbs flank steak
- Salt and pepper

Chimichurri Sauce:

- 1 cup fresh parsley
- 2 garlic cloves
- 2 tbsp red wine vinegar
- 1/2 cup olive oil
- 1 tsp oregano
- 1/2 tsp red pepper flakes
- Salt to taste

Instructions:

1. Season steak with salt and pepper, grill over high heat 4–5 minutes per side. Rest and slice thin against the grain.
2. Blend chimichurri ingredients and serve generously over steak.

Garlic Butter Basted Steak

Ingredients:

- 2 steaks (your choice)
- Salt and pepper
- 3 tbsp butter
- 4 garlic cloves, smashed
- Fresh thyme or rosemary sprigs

Instructions:

1. Season steaks with salt and pepper. Sear on high heat 3–4 minutes per side.
2. Add butter, garlic, and herbs to pan; tilt pan and spoon butter over steaks repeatedly for 1–2 minutes.
3. Rest and serve.

Asian Marinated Steak

Ingredients:

- 1 lb flank or skirt steak

Marinade:

- 1/4 cup soy sauce
- 2 tbsp sesame oil
- 1 tbsp honey
- 2 garlic cloves, minced
- 1 tbsp grated ginger
- 2 green onions, chopped
- 1 tsp chili flakes (optional)

Instructions:

1. Marinate steak for 1–2 hours.
2. Grill or pan-fry 3–4 minutes per side for medium-rare.
3. Slice thin and serve over rice or noodles.

Blue Cheese Crusted Steak

Ingredients:

- 2 steaks (ribeye or sirloin)
- Salt and pepper
- 1/2 cup crumbled blue cheese
- 2 tbsp butter
- 1 tbsp olive oil

Instructions:

1. Season steaks and cook in a skillet 4–5 minutes per side for medium-rare.
2. In last minute, top each steak with blue cheese and cover pan to melt cheese.
3. Rest and serve.

Herb-Crusted Sirloin

Ingredients:

- 1 sirloin steak (1–1.5 inch thick)
- 2 tbsp chopped fresh rosemary
- 2 tbsp chopped fresh thyme
- 2 cloves garlic, minced
- Salt and pepper
- 2 tbsp olive oil

Instructions:

1. Mix herbs and garlic with olive oil. Pat onto both sides of steak.
2. Season with salt and pepper.
3. Grill or pan-sear 4–5 minutes per side for medium-rare. Rest before serving.

Stuffed Flank Steak

Ingredients:

- 1 flank steak (about 1.5 lbs), butterflied
- Salt and pepper
- 1 cup spinach, sautéed and drained
- 1/2 cup sun-dried tomatoes, chopped
- 1/2 cup mozzarella or feta cheese

Instructions:

1. Lay butterflied steak flat, season with salt and pepper.
2. Spread spinach, sun-dried tomatoes, and cheese evenly.
3. Roll steak tightly and secure with kitchen twine.
4. Sear roll in pan until browned all over, then finish in 375°F (190°C) oven for 10–15 minutes. Rest, slice, and serve.

Surf and Turf

Ingredients:

- 2 ribeye or filet steaks
- 8 large shrimp or lobster tails
- Salt and pepper
- 2 tbsp olive oil
- 2 tbsp butter
- 2 garlic cloves, minced
- Fresh lemon wedges

Instructions:

1. Season steaks with salt and pepper. Grill or pan-sear steaks 4–5 minutes per side for medium-rare. Rest.
2. Sauté shrimp or lobster in butter and garlic until cooked through, about 3–4 minutes.
3. Serve steak topped or sided with the seafood and lemon wedges.

Balsamic Glazed Steak

Ingredients:

- 2 steaks (sirloin or ribeye)
- Salt and pepper
- 1/4 cup balsamic vinegar
- 2 tbsp brown sugar
- 2 tbsp olive oil

Instructions:

1. Season steaks with salt and pepper. Grill or pan-sear 4 minutes per side. Rest.
2. In pan, reduce balsamic vinegar and brown sugar until syrupy.
3. Drizzle glaze over steaks before serving.

Grilled Ribeye with Rosemary

Ingredients:

- 2 ribeye steaks
- Salt and pepper
- 2 tbsp olive oil
- 2 sprigs fresh rosemary

Instructions:

1. Rub steaks with olive oil, salt, and pepper.
2. Grill over medium-high heat 4–5 minutes per side, adding rosemary sprigs on grill for aroma.
3. Rest steaks and serve.

Mushroom Sauce Steak

Ingredients:

- 2 steaks
- Salt and pepper
- 2 tbsp butter
- 1 cup mushrooms, sliced
- 1/4 cup shallots, minced
- 1/2 cup beef broth
- 1/4 cup heavy cream

Instructions:

1. Cook steaks 4 minutes per side, rest.
2. In same pan, sauté shallots and mushrooms in butter until soft.
3. Add broth and reduce, stir in cream until thickened.
4. Pour sauce over steaks to serve.

Teriyaki Glazed Steak

Ingredients:

- 2 flank steaks
- 1/4 cup soy sauce
- 2 tbsp mirin
- 2 tbsp sake
- 2 tbsp brown sugar
- 2 garlic cloves, minced
- 1 tsp grated ginger

Instructions:

1. Combine soy, mirin, sake, sugar, garlic, and ginger to make marinade.
2. Marinate steak 1–2 hours.
3. Grill or pan-fry 4–5 minutes per side. Brush with extra glaze while cooking. Rest before slicing.

Steak Salad with Arugula

Ingredients:

- 1 grilled steak, sliced thin
- 4 cups arugula
- 1/2 cup cherry tomatoes, halved
- 1/4 cup shaved Parmesan
- 2 tbsp olive oil
- 1 tbsp balsamic vinegar
- Salt and pepper

Instructions:

1. Toss arugula, tomatoes, Parmesan, olive oil, vinegar, salt, and pepper.
2. Top with warm sliced steak. Serve immediately.

Classic Steak Sandwich

Ingredients:

- 1 cooked steak, sliced thin
- 2 hoagie rolls or baguettes
- 1 cup sautéed onions and peppers
- 4 slices provolone or Swiss cheese
- 2 tbsp mayonnaise or horseradish sauce

Instructions:

1. Layer steak, sautéed veggies, and cheese on rolls.
2. Toast in oven until cheese melts. Spread mayo or horseradish on bread before assembling.

Jamaican Jerk Steak

Ingredients:

- 1 lb sirloin or ribeye steak

Jerk Marinade:

- 2 tbsp soy sauce
- 2 tbsp lime juice
- 1 tbsp brown sugar
- 1 tbsp allspice
- 1 tsp cinnamon
- 1 tsp thyme
- 2 garlic cloves, minced
- 1 Scotch bonnet pepper or substitute, minced (optional)
- Salt and pepper

Instructions:

1. Mix marinade ingredients, coat steak, and marinate at least 1 hour.
2. Grill steak over medium-high heat 4–5 minutes per side. Rest and serve.

Red Wine Braised Steak

Ingredients:

- 2 thick-cut steaks (chuck or blade)
- Salt and pepper
- 2 tbsp olive oil
- 1 onion, sliced
- 3 garlic cloves, minced
- 1 cup red wine
- 1 cup beef broth
- 2 sprigs thyme
- 1 bay leaf

Instructions:

1. Season steaks, sear in olive oil until browned on both sides. Remove and set aside.
2. Sauté onion and garlic in the same pan until soft.
3. Add red wine, beef broth, thyme, and bay leaf; bring to simmer.
4. Return steaks to pan, cover, and braise on low heat for 1.5–2 hours until tender.

Mediterranean Steak Skewers

Ingredients:

- 1 lb sirloin, cut into cubes
- 2 tbsp olive oil
- 1 tbsp lemon juice
- 2 garlic cloves, minced
- 1 tsp dried oregano
- Salt and pepper
- Cherry tomatoes, bell peppers, and red onion chunks for skewering

Instructions:

1. Marinate steak cubes in olive oil, lemon, garlic, oregano, salt, and pepper for 30 min.
2. Thread steak and veggies onto skewers.
3. Grill 3–4 minutes per side to desired doneness.

Wasabi Crusted Steak

Ingredients:

- 2 steaks (ribeye or sirloin)
- Salt and pepper
- 2 tbsp wasabi paste
- 1/2 cup panko breadcrumbs
- 2 tbsp mayonnaise

Instructions:

1. Mix wasabi and mayonnaise, spread on top of steaks.
2. Press panko breadcrumbs over wasabi layer.
3. Broil steaks 3–4 minutes until crust is golden. Rest and serve.

Steak with Béarnaise Sauce

Ingredients:

- 2 steaks (your choice)
- Salt and pepper

Béarnaise Sauce:

- 3 egg yolks
- 1/4 cup white wine vinegar
- 1/4 cup white wine
- 2 tbsp chopped tarragon
- 1 shallot, minced
- 1/2 cup melted butter
- Salt and pepper

Instructions:

1. Cook steaks to preferred doneness and rest.
2. Simmer vinegar, wine, shallot, and half tarragon until reduced by half.
3. Strain, whisk into egg yolks over double boiler until thick.
4. Slowly whisk in melted butter. Add salt, pepper, and remaining tarragon.
5. Serve sauce over steak.

Pepper Steak Stir Fry

Ingredients:

- 1 lb flank steak, thinly sliced
- 2 bell peppers, sliced
- 1 onion, sliced
- 3 garlic cloves, minced
- 2 tbsp soy sauce
- 1 tbsp oyster sauce
- 1 tsp cornstarch mixed with 2 tbsp water
- 2 tbsp vegetable oil

Instructions:

1. Stir-fry steak in oil until browned; remove.
2. Stir-fry peppers, onion, and garlic until crisp-tender.
3. Return steak to pan; add soy, oyster sauce, and cornstarch slurry.
4. Cook until sauce thickens. Serve over rice.

Garlic and Thyme Steak

Ingredients:

- 2 steaks
- Salt and pepper
- 3 garlic cloves, crushed
- 2 sprigs fresh thyme
- 2 tbsp butter
- 2 tbsp olive oil

Instructions:

1. Season steaks, sear in olive oil 4–5 minutes per side.
2. Add butter, garlic, and thyme; baste steaks with melted butter.
3. Rest and serve.

Grilled Flat Iron Steak

Ingredients:

- 1 lb flat iron steak
- 2 tbsp olive oil
- Salt and pepper
- 1 tsp smoked paprika
- 1 tsp garlic powder

Instructions:

1. Rub steak with olive oil, salt, pepper, paprika, and garlic powder.
2. Grill over high heat 4–5 minutes per side for medium rare. Rest before slicing.

Steak Tacos

Ingredients:

- 1 lb flank steak, grilled and sliced thin
- Corn or flour tortillas
- 1/2 cup chopped onion
- 1/2 cup chopped cilantro
- Lime wedges
- Salsa or hot sauce

Instructions:

1. Warm tortillas.
2. Fill with steak slices, onion, and cilantro.
3. Serve with lime wedges and salsa.

Asian Beef Bulgogi Steak

Ingredients:

- 1 lb thinly sliced sirloin or ribeye
- 1/4 cup soy sauce
- 2 tbsp brown sugar
- 1 tbsp sesame oil
- 3 garlic cloves, minced
- 1 tsp grated ginger
- 2 green onions, chopped
- 1 tbsp gochujang (Korean chili paste) (optional)
- 1 tsp toasted sesame seeds

Instructions:

1. Mix soy sauce, sugar, sesame oil, garlic, ginger, green onions, and gochujang.
2. Marinate beef slices at least 30 minutes.
3. Cook quickly on high heat in a skillet or grill until just cooked.
4. Sprinkle with sesame seeds and serve.

Montreal Smoked Steak

Ingredients:

- 2 steaks (ribeye or striploin)
- 2 tbsp Montreal steak spice
- 1 tbsp olive oil

Instructions:

1. Rub steaks with olive oil and Montreal steak spice.
2. Smoke on a grill or smoker at low heat (~225°F) for 45–60 minutes until desired doneness.
3. Optional: Sear on high heat after smoking for crust.

Spicy Chipotle Steak

Ingredients:

- 2 steaks (flank or skirt)
- 2 tbsp chipotle chili powder
- 1 tsp smoked paprika
- 1 tsp garlic powder
- Salt and pepper
- 2 tbsp olive oil

Instructions:

1. Mix chipotle chili powder, paprika, garlic powder, salt, and pepper.
2. Rub steaks with olive oil and spice mix.
3. Grill or pan-sear 4–5 minutes per side.

Lemon Garlic Steak

Ingredients:

- 2 steaks
- 3 garlic cloves, minced
- Juice and zest of 1 lemon
- 2 tbsp olive oil
- Salt and pepper
- Fresh parsley, chopped

Instructions:

1. Mix garlic, lemon juice/zest, olive oil, salt, and pepper.
2. Marinate steaks 30 minutes.
3. Grill or pan-fry steaks, basting with marinade.
4. Sprinkle parsley before serving.

Herb Butter Sirloin

Ingredients:

- 2 sirloin steaks
- Salt and pepper
- 3 tbsp unsalted butter
- 1 tbsp mixed chopped fresh herbs (thyme, rosemary, parsley)
- 2 garlic cloves, crushed

Instructions:

1. Cook steaks to desired doneness.
2. Melt butter with herbs and garlic, spoon over steaks before serving.

Japanese Wagyu Steak

Ingredients:

- 1 Wagyu steak (ribeye or sirloin)
- Sea salt
- Freshly ground black pepper
- Wasabi (optional)

Instructions:

1. Let steak reach room temp.
2. Lightly season with salt and pepper.
3. Sear quickly on high heat to rare or medium-rare (Wagyu is best enjoyed less cooked).
4. Serve with a small dab of wasabi.

Black Garlic Butter Steak

Ingredients:

- 2 steaks
- 3 tbsp unsalted butter
- 1 tbsp black garlic paste
- Salt and pepper

Instructions:

1. Cook steaks to desired doneness.
2. Mix butter and black garlic paste.
3. Spoon over hot steaks before serving.

Coffee and Chili Rubbed Steak

Ingredients:

- 2 steaks
- 1 tbsp ground coffee
- 1 tsp chili powder
- 1 tsp smoked paprika
- 1 tsp brown sugar
- Salt and pepper

Instructions:

1. Mix coffee, chili powder, paprika, sugar, salt, and pepper.
2. Rub on steaks.
3. Grill or pan-sear 4–5 minutes per side.

Rosemary Garlic Ribeye

Ingredients:

- 2 ribeye steaks
- 2 tbsp olive oil
- 3 garlic cloves, smashed
- 2 sprigs rosemary
- Salt and pepper

Instructions:

1. Season steaks with salt and pepper.
2. Sear steaks in olive oil, add garlic and rosemary to pan.
3. Baste steaks with flavored oil while cooking.
4. Rest and serve.

Truffle Butter Steak

Ingredients:

- 2 steaks
- Salt and pepper
- 3 tbsp truffle butter (butter mixed with truffle oil or shaved truffle)

Instructions:

1. Cook steaks to your liking.
2. Top immediately with a dollop of truffle butter.
3. Let butter melt and serve.